P9-CLL-747

P9-CLL-747

THE NORMAN ROCKWELL

Family Songbook

THE NORMAN ROCKWELL
Family Songbook

arranged for piano and guitar by

Stephen Dydo and Randa Kirshbaum

with illustrations by Norman Rockwell

Harry N. Abrams, Inc., Publishers, New York

Courtesy Massachusetts
Mutual Life Insurance Company

The Publishers wish to thank Marvin Jones of
The New York Public Library (Music Research Division)
for his invaluable assistance.

Music engraving by The Music Factory

Project Manager: Lois Brown
Editor: Ruth Eisenstein
Designer: Darilyn Lowe

Library of Congress Catalog Card Number: 84-70537

ISBN 0-8109-1561-8 (cloth)
ISBN 0-8109-2289-4 (paper)

©1984 Harry N. Abrams, Inc., New York

Published in 1984 by Harry N. Abrams, Incorporated, New York
All rights reserved. No part of the contents of this book may be
reproduced without the written permission of the publishers

Printed and bound in the United States of America

Contents

American Favorites

The Sidewalks of New York

Moderate waltz

Down in front of Ca - sey's _____ Old brown
That's where John - ny Ca - sey _____ And Lit - tle
Things have changed since those times, _____ Some are

wood - en stoop, _____ On a sum - mer's
Jim - my Crowe, _____ With Jak - ey Kraus, ___ the
up ___ in "G," _____ Oth - ers, they ___ are

eve - ning, _____ We formed a mer - ry group; _____
bak - er _____ Who al - ways had the dough; _____
wan - d'rers _____ But they all feel just like me; _____

Boys and girls to - geth - er, ———— we would
Pret - ty Nel - lie Shan - non, ———— with a dude as
They'd part with all they've got ———— could they

sing —— and waltz, ———— While To - ny played the
light —— as cork, ———— first picked up the
once —— more walk ———— with their best girl and

or - gan on the side - walks of New York.
waltz - step on the side - walks of New York.
have a twirl on the side - walks of New York.

East side, West side, all a - round the

12

town, _____ The tots sang "ring - a - ro - sie," "Lon - don Bridge is

fal - ling down." _____ Boys and girls to - geth - er, _____

Me and Ma - mie O' - Rorke , _____ Tripped the light _ fan - tas - tic

on the side - walks of New York.   York.

Yankee Doodle

YANKEE DOODLE CAME TO TO[WN]

Lively

1. Oh, Yan - kee Doodle went to town, u - pon a lit - tle po - ny. He
2. Father and I went down to camp, a - long with Cap - tain Good - win, And

stuck a fea - ther in his cap And call'd it ma - ca - ro - ni.
there we saw the men and boys, As thick as hast - y pud - din'.

RIDING ON A PONY · STUCK A FEATHER IN HIS HAT · AND CALLED IT MACARONI

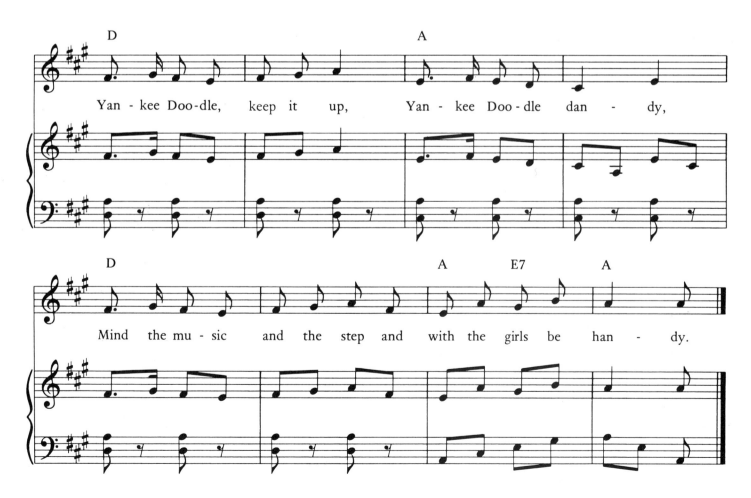

Yan - kee Doo-dle, keep it up, Yan - kee Doo - dle dan - dy,

Mind the mu - sic and the step and with the girls be han - dy.

Give My Regards to Broadway

Words and music by George M. Cohan

Bright march

1. Did you ev - er see two Yan - kees part up - on a for - eign shore, _____ When the good ship's just a - bout to start for

2. Say hel - lo to dear old Co - ney Isle, if on there you chance to be, _____ When you're at the Wal - dorf, have a smile for and

16

Whis-per of how I'm yearn - ing to

min - gle with the old time throng; ⸺

Give my re - gards to old Broad - way and say that I'll be

there, e'er long. long. ⸺

Simple Gifts

Moderately

'Tis a gift to be sim-ple, 'tis a gift to be free, 'Tis a gift to come down where we ought to be, And when we find our-selves in the place just right, 'Twill be in the val-ley of love and de-light. When true sim-

C

pli - ci - ty is gained, To bow and to bend we___ shan't be a - shamed. To

F

turn, turn, will be our de-light, Till by turn - ing, turn - ing we come 'round right.

Midnight Special

see the same damn thing.   Well, it's on-ly one
and you bet-ter not fight.   'Cause the sher-iff will ar -

ta - ble, _____ knife and fork and a pan,
rest you, _____ and he'll car-ry you down,

And if you say a thing a-bout it, _____ you're in trou-ble with the man.
And you can bet your bot-tom dol lar, _____ you're for Su - gar-land bound.

Chorus:

Let the Mid - night Spe - cial _____ shine her light on

23

3. Lord, Thelma said she loved me, but I believe she told a lie,
   'Cause she hasn't been to see me since last July.
   She brought me little coffee, she brought me little tea,
   She brought me nearly everything but the jail house key.

Shenandoah

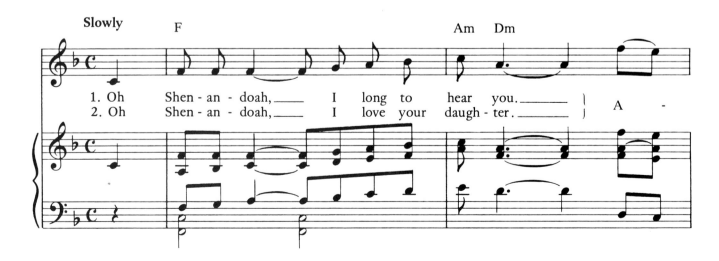

1. Oh Shen - an - doah,____ I long to hear you.____
2. Oh Shen - an - doah,____ I love your daugh - ter.____

3. Oh Shenandoah, I'm bound to leave you,
   Chorus: Away, you rolling river.
   Oh Shenandoah, I'll not deceive you,
   Chorus: Away I'm bound to go,
        'Cross the wide Missouri.

4. Oh Shenandoah, I long to hear you,
   Chorus: Away, you rolling river.
   Oh Shenandoah, I long to hear you,
   Chorus: Away I'm bound to go,
        'Cross the wide Missouri.

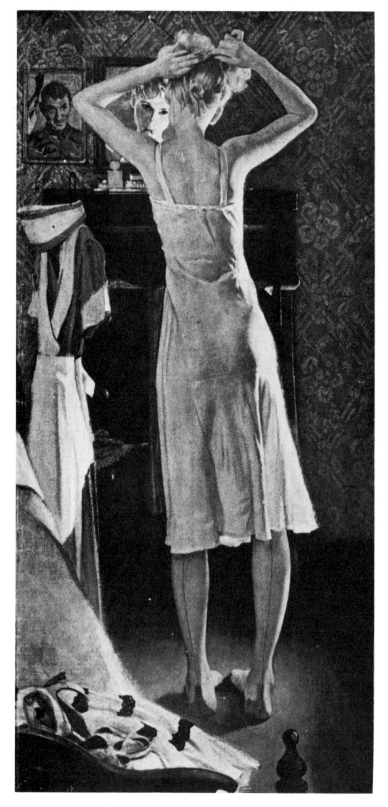

The Band Played On

Words by C. B. Ward
Music by J. F. Palmer

line   Be - hind the man who was their joy and   pride. _____

floor   Is   hap - py   mis - sus   Ca - sey now for   life. _____

Chorus:

For _____   Ca - sey would waltz with a   straw - ber - ry

blond and the   band   played   on, _____   He'd

glide cross the floor with the   girl he a - dor'd and the   band

played on, _____ But his brain was so load-ed it

near-ly ex-plod-ed, the poor girl would shake with a-larm. _____

___ He'd ne'er leave the girl with the straw-ber-ry curls, And the

band played on. on. _____

On Top of Old Smokey

Oh, Susanna!

Words and music by Stephen Foster

1. I come from A - la - ba - ma with my ban - jo on my knee, I'm going to Louis - i - a - na, My Su - san - na for to see.
2. It rained all day the night I left, The weath - er it was dry, The sun so hot I froze my - self, Su - san - na don't you cry.

Chorus:

Oh, Su - san - na! Oh, don't you cry for me, For I

come from A - la - ba - ma with my ban - jo on my knee.

3. I had a dream the other night,
   When everything was still.
   I thought I saw Susanna
   A-comin' down the hill.

4. The red, red rose was in her hand,
   The tear was in her eye,
   I said, "I come from Dixie Land,
   Susanna, don't you cry."

The Blue-Tail Fly

Slowly and freely

1. When I was young I used to wait On mas-ter and give him his plate, And
2. When he rode in the af-ter-noon I'd fol-low him with hick-'ry broom,The

accel.

pass the bot-tle when he got dry, And brush a - way the blue-tail fly.
po - ny, be - ing ra - ther shy When bit - ten by the blue-tail fly.

Chorus:
Lively

Jim-my crack corn and I don't care, Jim-my crack corn and I don't care,

F   Bb   C7   F

Jim-my crack corn and I don't care, My mas-ter's gone a - way.

3. Once when he rode around the farm
   The flies about him thick did swarm,
   The pony which was very shy
   Was bitten by the blue-tail fly.

4. The pony run, he jump, he pitch,
   He throw my master in a ditch;
   He died and the jury wondered why;
   The verdict was, "The blue-tail fly!"

5. They laid him 'neath a 'simmon tree,
   His epitaph is there to see:
   "Beneath this stone I'm forced to lie,
   A victim of the blue-tail fly."

Arkansas Traveler

Words by David Stevens

1. Oh once up-on a time in Ar - kan-sas, an old man sat in his lit - tle cab-in door, And fid - dled at a tune that he liked to hear, A jol - ly old tune that he play'd by ear. It was rain - ing hard, but the

2. A trav - el - er was rid - ing by that day, And stopped to hear him a - prac - tic - ing a - way; The cab - in was a - float and his feet were wet, But still the old man did - n't seem to fret. So the strang - er said: "Now the

Lyrics by David Stevens © 1920, C.C. Birchard & Co. Used by permission of Summy-Birchard Music Division of Birch Tree Group Ltd.

fid - dler did - n't care, He saw'd a - way at the pop - u - lar air, Tho' his
way it seems to me, You'd bet - ter mend your_ roof," said he. But the

roof tree leak'd like a wa - ter - fall, That did - n't seem to bo - ther the man_ at all.
old man said, as he played a - way: "I could - n't mend it now, it's a rain - y day."

3. The traveler replied: "That's all quite true,
But this, I think, is the thing for you to do;
Get busy on a day that is fair and bright,
Then patch the old roof till it's good and tight."
But the old man kept on a-playing at his reel,
And tapp'd the ground with his leathery heel:
"Get along," said he, "for you give me a pain;
My cabin never leaks when it doesn't rain."

My Old Kentucky Home

Words and music by Stephen Foster

Bill Bailey, Won't You Please Come Home?

Lively

F

Words and music by Hughie Cannon

"Won't you come home, Bill Bai - ley, won't you come home?"

C7

She cried the whole night long. "I'll do the

Bb

dish - es, hon - ey, I'll pay the rent. I know I done you

wrong.   'Mem - ber   that   rain - y   eve - ning

I   drove   you   out   With   noth-in'   but   a   fine - tooth   comb?

—   I   know   I'm   to   blame,   Well   ain't   that   a

shame?   Bill   Bai - ley, won't you   please   come   home?"

Swinging on a Star

Words by Johnny Burke
Music by Jimmy Van Heusen

Copyright © 1944 (Renewed) by Dorsey Bros. Music, a Division of Music Sales Corp., New York, and Burke and Van Heusen, a Division of Bourne Company, New York. All Rights Reserved. Used by Permission.

1. A mule is an an-i-mal with long fun-ny ears, He kicks up at an-y-thing he
2. A pig is an an-i-mal with dirt on his face, His shoes are a ter-ri-ble dis-

hears,_____ His back is brawn-y and his brain is weak,__ He's
grace,_____ He's got no man-ners when he eats his food,__ He's

just plain stu-pid with a stub-born streak And by the way, if you hate to go to
fat and la-zy and ex-treme-ly rude, But if you don't care a feath-er or a

school, you may grow up to be a mule._____
fig, you may grow up to be a pig._____ } Or would you

like to swing on a star, Car-ry moon-beams home in a jar, _____ And be

bet - ter off than you are, Or would you ra - ther be a

1., 2.   3.

1. pig?   A   are,   You could be swing-ing on a star.
2. fish?   A

The Camptown Races

Words and music by Stephen Foster

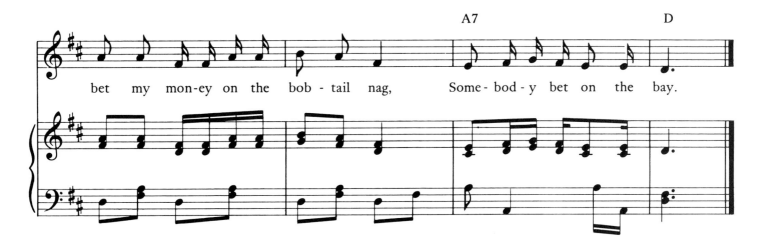

bet my mon-ey on the bob - tail nag, Some - bod - y bet on the bay.

2. The long tail filly and the big black horse, doo-dah, doo-dah,
They flew the track, and both cut across, Oh, doo-dah day.
The blind horse sticking in a big mud hole, doo-dah, doo-dah,
Couldn't touch bottom with a ten-foot pole, Oh, doo-dah day.

Dixie

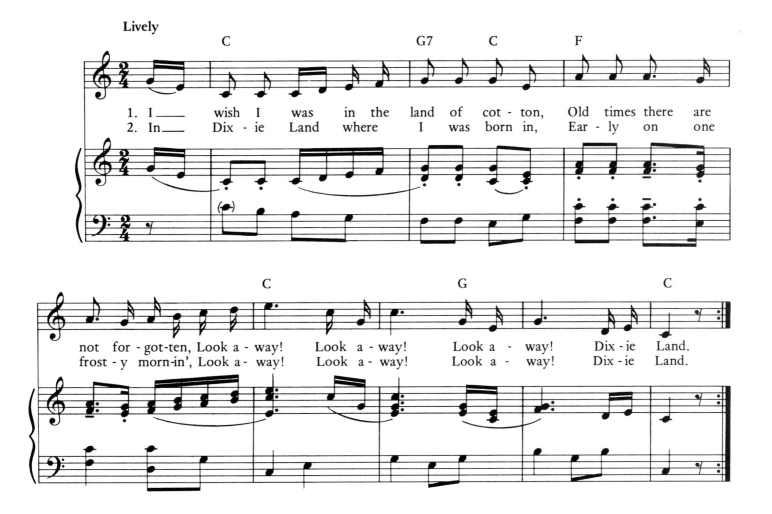

1. I____ wish I was in the land of cot - ton, Old times there are
2. In____ Dix - ie Land where I was born in, Ear - ly on one

not for - got-ten, Look a - way! Look a - way! Look a - way! Dix - ie Land.
frost - y morn-in', Look a - way! Look a - way! Look a - way! Dix - ie Land.

Chorus:

Then I wish I was in Dix - ie, Hoo - ray! Hoo - ray! In Dix - ie Land I'll

take my stand, To live and die in Dix - ie; A - way, a - way, a -

way down south in Dix - ie, A - way, a - way, a - way down south in Dix - ie.

3. There's buckwheat cakes and Injun batter,
   Makes you fat or a little fatter,
   Look away! Look away! Look away! Dixie Land.

4. Then hoe it down and scratch your gravel,
   To Dixie Land I'm bound to travel,
   Look away! Look away! Look away! Dixie Land.

48

Work Songs

Haul Away, Joe

With heavy accents

1. Way, haul a - way, _____ we'll haul a - way the bow - lin' _____
2. Once I had a Span - ish girl, she near - ly drove me cra - zy. _____

Chorus:

Way, haul a - way, _____ we'll haul a - way, Joe. _____

3. But now I've got a Yankee girl, and she is just a daisy.
4. King Louis was the King of France afore the revolution.
5. But Louis got his head cut off, which spoiled his constitution.
6. Oh, when I was a little boy, and so my mother told me,
7. That if I didn't kiss the girls my lips would all go moldy.
8. Way, haul away, we'll hang and haul together.

51

Drill, Ye Tarriers, Drill!

Words and music by Thomas Casey

With heavy accents

1. Ev - 'ry mor - ning at sev - en o - 'clock There were twen - ty tar - ri - ers a -

work-in' at the rock, And the boss comes a - long, and he says, keep still, And

come down hea - vy on the cast i - ron drill, And drill, ye tar - ri - ers, drill!

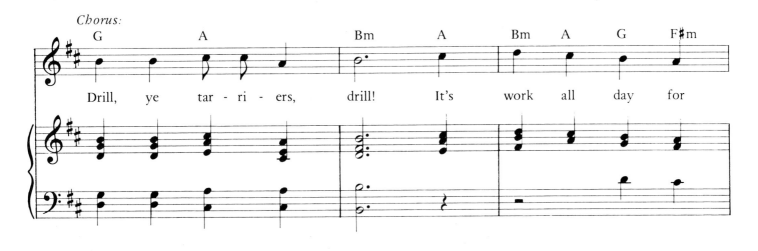

Drill, ye tar-ri-ers, drill! It's work all day for

su-gar in your tay, Down be-hind of the rail-way, And

drill, ye tar-ri-ers, drill, and blast! and fire!

2. The new foreman was Jim McCann,
   By God, he was a blame mean man!
   Last week an early blast went off,
   And a mile in the air went big Jim Goff,
   And drill, ye tarriers, drill!

3. When next the pay-day came around,
   Jim Goff a dollar short was found.
   "What for?" he asked, came this reply:
   "You're docked for the time you was up in the sky."
   And drill, ye tarriers, drill!

The Farmer Is the Man

Moderately

1. When the farm-er comes to town With his wag-on bro-ken down Oh, the
2. When the law-yer hangs a-round While the butch-er cuts a pound,

farm-er is the man who feeds them all.

If you'll on-ly look and see, I ____
And the preach-er and the cook Go a

think you will a-gree That the farm-er is the man who feeds them all.
stroll-ing by the brook, Oh, the farm-er is the man who feeds them all.

Chorus:

The

farm-er is the man, ___ The farm-er is the man, lives on cred-it till the

fall;

{ Then they take him by the hand, And they
{ With the int' - rest rate so high, It's a

lead him from the land, And the mid-dle man's the one who gets it all.
won-der he don't die, For the mort-gage man's the one who gets it all.

The Rock Island Line

If you ev-er want to ride it, got to ride it like you're

fly-in'. Buy your tic-ket on the sta-tion on the Rock Is-land Line. _____

1.   A,   B,   C,   dou - ble   X,   Y,   Z,
2. Now Je - sus   died   to   save   our   sins,
3. I   may   be   right   and   I   may   be   wrong,   I

Cat's   in   the   cup - board,   but   he   can't   see   me. _____
Glo - ry   be   to   God,   we're   gon - na   need   Him   a - gain. _____
know   you're gon - na   miss   me   when   I   am   gone. _____

58

Molly Malone

Cock - les and mus - sels a - live, a - live Oh!"

Chorus:

"A - live, a - live oh, __ a - live, a - live oh!"__ Cry - ing

"Cock - les and mus - sels a - live, a - live oh!"

Blow the Man Down

Give me some time to blow the man down!

3. She was round in the center
   and bluff in the bow,
   Chorus
   So I took in all sail and cried,
   "Way 'nough now."
   Chorus

4. So I tailed her my flipper and
   took her in tow,
   Chorus
   And yardarm to yardarm
   away we did go.
   Chorus

5. But as we were going she said
   unto me,
   Chorus
   "There's a spanking full-rigger
   just ready for sea."
   Chorus

6. But as soon as that packet was
   clear of the bar,
   Chorus
   The mate knocked me down
   with the end of a spar.
   Chorus

7. So I give you fair warning
   before we belay,
   Chorus
   Don't take a heed of what
   pretty girls say.
   Chorus

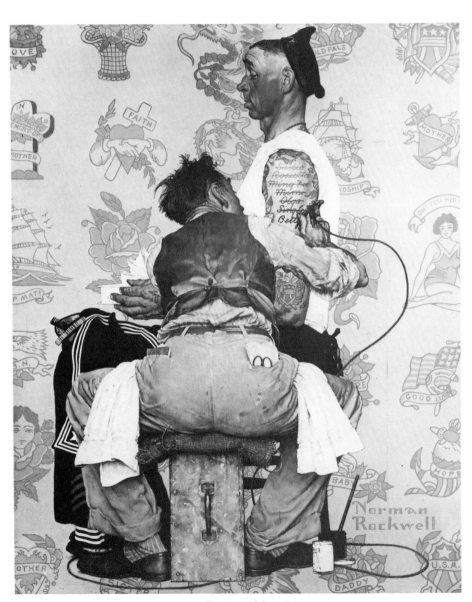

Courtesy The Brooklyn Museum

John Henry

1. When John Henry was a lit-tle ba - by sit - tin' on his pa - pa's knee, Well, he took a ham-mer, lit-tle piece of steel, say-in' hammer gonna be the death of me

2. When John Henry was a lit-tle ba - by sit - tin' on his mo - ma's knee, Said the Big Bend Tun-nel on the C & O Road gon-na be the death of me

Em

Lord, Lord,— the ham-mer gon-na be the death of - a me.—
Lord, Lord,— gon' be _____ the death of - a me.—

3. John Henry had a little woman,
   Her name was Mary Magdalene.
   Every day she would sing for John Henry
   Just to hear his hammer when it swing, Lord, Lord,
   Just to hear his hammer when it swing.

4. And now the captain, he says to John Henry,
   "I'm gonna bring that steam drill round,
   I'm gonna bring that steam drill out on the job,
   I'm gonna whop that steel on down, Lord, Lord,
   Gonna whop that steel on down."

5. John Henry said to his captain,
   "I know a man ain't nothin' but a man,
   But before I let your steam drill beat me down,
   I'll die with my hammer in my hand, Lord, Lord,
   I'll die with my hammer in my hand."

6. John Henry said to his shaker,
   "Shaker, why don't you sing?
   And now I'm throwin' forty pounds from my hip on down,
   Listen to that cold steel ring, Lord, Lord,
   Listen to that cold steel ring."

7. John Henry said to his captain,
   "Look-a yonder what I see—
   Steam drill broke, your hole done choke,
   You can't drive steel like me, Lord, Lord,
   You can't drive steel like me."

8. John Henry a-workin' on the mountain,
   Hammer was a-strikin' fire,
   But he work so hard it broke his heart,
   And he laid down his hammer and he died, Lord, Lord,
   He laid down his hammer and he died.

The Erie Canal

Jaunty

1. We were for - ty miles from Al - ba - ny, For - get it I ne - ver shall, What a ter - ri -ble storm we had one night on the E - ri - e* Ca - nal.

Chorus: Oh the E - ri - e was a - ris - ing, The gin was get - ting

* The word. "E-ri-e" in this song is pronounced "Ee-rye-ee".

2. We were loaded down with barley,
   We were chuck up full of rye;
   And the captain he looked down at me
   With his goddam wicked eye.

Chorus:

3. Oh the girls are in the Police Gazette,
   The crew are all in jail;
   I'm the only living sea cook's son
   That's left to tell the tale.

Chorus:

a Family Tree by norman rockwell

Riddle Song

In the Good Old Summer Time

Words and music by Ren Shields and George Evans

In the

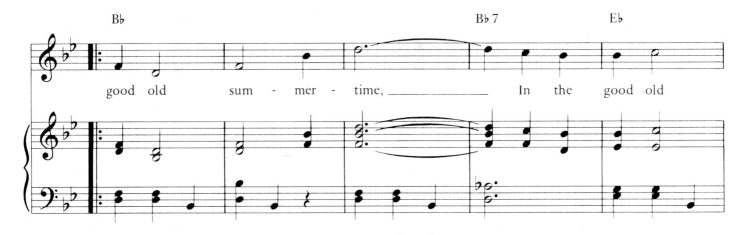

good old sum - mer - time, _____ In the good old

sum - mer - time, _____ Stroll - ing through the

Personality

Words by Johnny Burke
Music by Jimmy Van Heusen

Copyright © 1945 (Renewed) by Dorsey Bros. Music, a Division of Music Sales Corp., New York, and Burke and Van Heusen, a Division of Bourne Company, New York. All Rights Reserved. Used by Permission.

Jun - o? You know! _____ And when Sa -
spats right? That's right! _____ So, don't you

lo - me danced and had the boys en-tranced No doubt it must have been eas - y to see _
say I'm smart and have the kind-est heart, _ Or what a won-der-ful sis - ter I'd be _

That she knew how to use her
Just tell me how you like my

PER - SON-AL - I - TY. _____ A girl can
PER - SON-AL - I - TY: _____

Hush, Little Baby

Gently, like a lullaby

1. Hush, lit-tle ba - by, don't say a word, Pa-pa's gon-na buy you a mock-ing bird.
2. If that dia-mond ring turns brass, Pa-pa's gon-na buy you a look-ing glass.

If that mock-ing bird won't sing, Pa-pa's gon-na buy you a dia-mond ring.
If that look-ing glass gets broke, Pa-pa's gon-na buy you a bil - ly goat.

3. If that billy goat won't pull,
   Papa's gonna buy you a cart and bull.
   If that cart and bull turn over,
   Papa's gonna buy you a dog named Rover.

4. If that dog named Rover won't bark,
   Papa's gonna buy you a horse and cart.
   If that horse and cart fall down,
   You'll be the sweetest little baby in town.

Silver Threads Among the Gold

Words by Eben E. Rexford
Music by   H. P. Danks

be,   will be   Al - ways young and fair to   me,
lone,   a - lone,   You   have nev - er old - er   grown.

Yes!   my dar - ling, you will be _____   Al - ways young and fair to me.
Yes!   my dar - ling, mine a - lone, _____   You   have nev - er old - er   grown.

Chorus:

Dar - ling, I am grow-ing, grow - ing old,   Sil - ver threads a - mong the gold,

Shine up - on my brow to - day; _____   Life is fad - ing fast a - way.

All Through the Night

1. Sleep, my child and peace at-tend thee, All through the night; Guar-dian an-gels God will send thee, All through the night; Soft the drow-sy hours are creep-ing,

Hill and vale in slum - ber steep - ing; I my lov - ing
vi - gil keep - ing, All through the night.

2. While the moon her watch is keeping
   All through the night;
   While the weary world is sleeping
   All through the night;
   O'er thy spirit gently stealing,
   Visions of delight revealing,
   Breathes a pure and holy feeling
   All through the night.

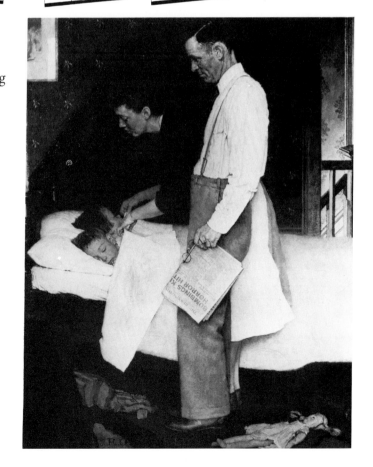

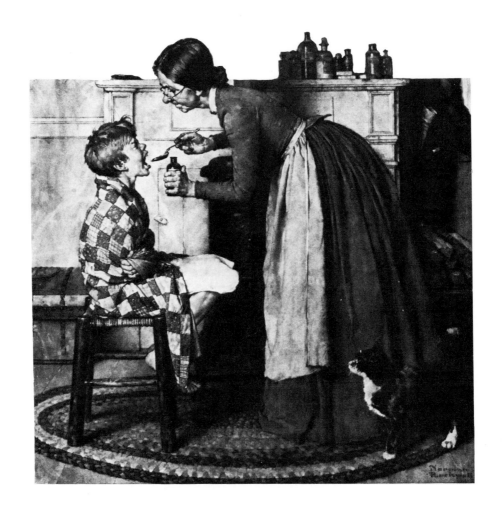

Hello Central, Give Me Heaven

Words and music by Charles K. Harris

Hel-lo Cen-tral, give me heav-en, For my ma-ma's there,

Courtesy Brown & Bigelow © 1953

When You and I Were Young, Maggie

Words and music by George W. Johnson and James A. Butterfield

I wan - dered to - day to the hill, Mag - gie, to watch the scene be - low; The creek and the old rus - ty

Old Folks at Home

Words and music by Stephen Foster

1.Way down u-pon the Swan-ee riv-er, Far, far a-way,
All up and down the whole cre-a-tion, Sad-ly I roam,

There's where my heart is turn ing ev-er; There's where the old folks___ stay.
Still long-ing for the old plan-ta-tion, And for the old folks at home.

Chorus:

All the world is sad and drear-y Ev'-ry where I roam,

O broth-ers, how my heart grows wear-y, Far from the old folks at home.

2. All around the little farm I wandered when I was young,
   There many happy days I've squandered, there many songs I've sung.
   When I was playing with my brother, happy was I,
   Oh, take me to my kind old mother, there let me live and die.

3. One little hut among the bushes, one that I love,
   Still sadly to my memory rushes, no matter where I rove.
   When will I see the bees a-humming all around the comb,
   When will I hear the banjo tumming, down in my good old home?

Kentucky Babe

Words by Richard Henry Buck
Music by Adam Geibel

Western Songs

Home on the Range

Home, home on the range, _____ Where the deer and the an-te-lope play; _____ Where

sel-dom is heard a dis-cour-ag-ing word, And the skies are not cloud-y all day. _____

3. Oh, I love those wild flowers in this dear land of ours,
The curlew, I love to hear scream,
And I love the white rocks and the antelope flocks
That graze on the mountain so green.

4. Where the air is so pure and the zephyrs so free,
The breezes so balmy and light
That I would not exchange my home on the range
For all of the cities so bright.

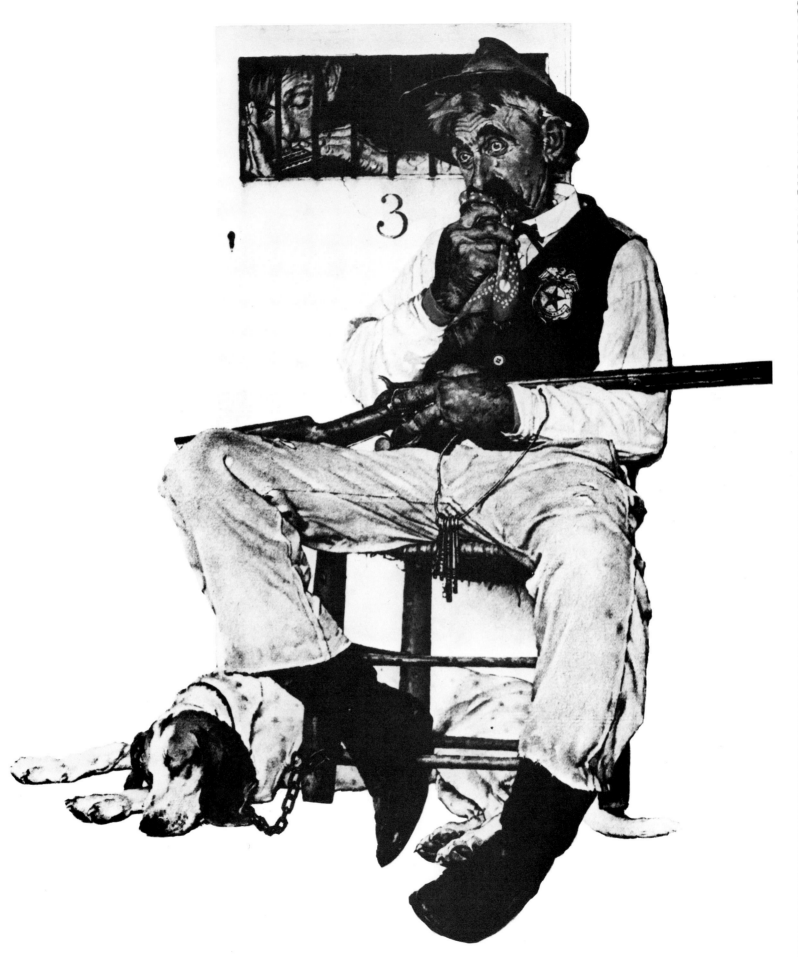

The Streets of Laredo

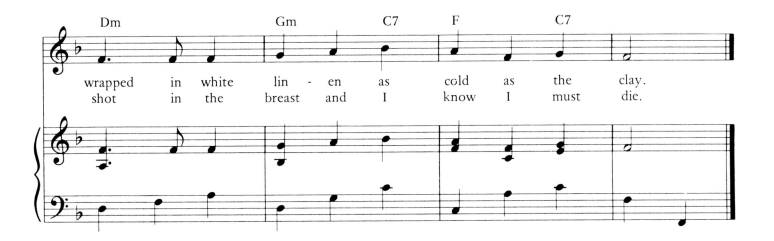

wrapped   in   white   lin - en   as   cold   as   the   clay.

shot   in   the   breast   and   I   know   I   must   die.

3. " 'Twas once in the saddle I used to go dashing,
    'Twas once in the saddle I used to go gay;
    'Twas first to go drinking, and then to card playing,
    Got shot in the breast and I'm dying today."

4. "Get six jolly cowboys to carry my coffin,
    Get six pretty maidens to carry my pall;
    Put bunches of roses all over my coffin,
    Roses to deaden the clods as they fall."

5. "Oh, beat the drum slowly, and play the fife lowly,
    And play the dead march as you bear me along;
    Take me to the valley and lay the sod o'er me,
    For I'm a young cowboy and I know I've done wrong."

6. We beat the drum slowly and played the fife lowly,
    And bitterly wept as we bore him along,
    For we loved our comrade, so brave, young, and handsome,
    We all loved our comrade although he'd done wrong.

The Yellow Rose of Texas

If we ev - er meet a - gain We nev - er more will part.
prom - ised to come back a - gain And nev - er leave me so."
lit - tle gal in Tex - as, She'll be mine for - ev - er more.

Chorus:

She's the sweet - est rose of col - or this sol - dier ev - er knew, Her eyes are bright as

dia - monds, they spar - kle like the dew. You may talk a - bout your dear - est May and

sing of Ro - sa Lee, But the Yel - low Rose of Tex - as is the on - ly girl for me.

Buffalo Gals

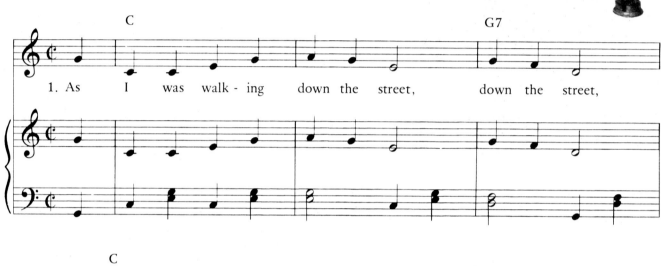

1. As I was walk-ing down the street, down the street,

down the street, A pret-ty lit-tle girl I chanced to meet, and we

danced by the light of the moon. Buf-fa-lo gals won't you come out to-night,

come out to - night come out to - night? Buf - fa - lo gals won't you

come out to - night, and dance by the light of the moon?

2. I asked her if she'd stop and talk, stop and talk, stop and talk,
   Her feet took up the whole sidewalk, and left no room for me.

3. I asked her if she'd be my wife, be my wife, be my wife,
   Then I'd be happy all my life, if she'd marry me.

Bury Me Not on the Lone Prairie

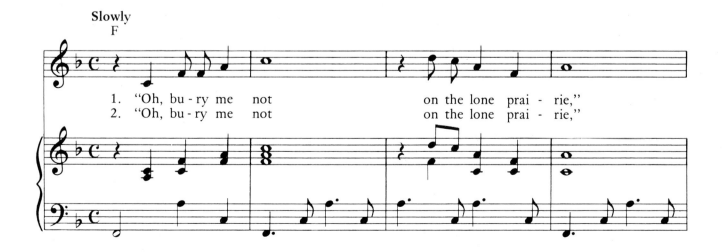

1. "Oh, bu - ry me not   on the lone prai - rie,"
2. "Oh, bu - ry me not   on the lone prai - rie,"

3. "I've always wished to be laid when I died
   In the little churchyard on the green hillside;
   By my father's grave there let mine be,
   And bury me not on the lone prairie."

4. "Oh, bury me not"— and his voice failed there,
   But we took no heed of his dying prayer.
   In a narrow grave, just six by three,
   We buried him on the lone prairie.

5. And the cowboys now, as they roam the plain,
   (For they marked the spot where his bones were lain),
   Fling a handful of roses over the grave,
   With a prayer to Him who his soul will save.

6. "Oh, bury me not on the lone prairie,
   Where the wolves can howl and growl o'er me.
   Fling a handful of roses over my grave,
   With a prayer to Him who my soul will save."

I Ride an Old Paint

I ride an old paint and I lead an old Dan, I'm
goin' to Mon - ta - na to throw the hoo - li - han. They
feed 'em in the cou - lees, they wa - ter in the draw, their

105

tails are all mat-ted their backs are all raw. Ride a-

round lit-tle dog-gies ride a-round _____ them _ slow, for the

Fier-y and Snuf-fy are rar-ing to go.

Sweet Betsy from Pike

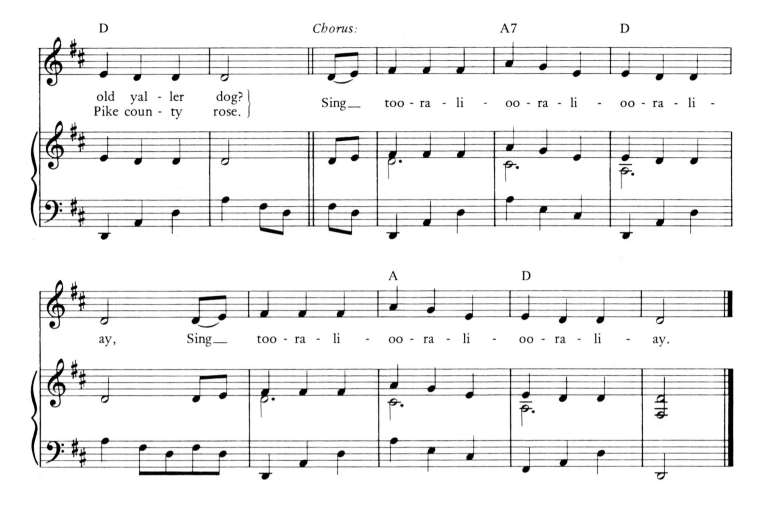

old yal - ler dog?}
Pike coun - ty rose.}

Sing__ too - ra - li - oo - ra - li - oo - ra - li -

ay, Sing__ too - ra - li - oo - ra - li - oo - ra - li - ay.

3. They swam the wide rivers and crossed the tall peaks,
And camped on the prairie for weeks upon weeks,
Starvation and cholera and hard work and slaughter,
They reached California spite of hell and high water.

4. Out on the prairie one bright starry night
They broke out the whiskey and Betsy got tight,
She sang and she shouted and danced o'er the plain,
And showed her bare arse to the whole wagon train.

5. The Injuns came down in a wild yelling horde,
And Betsy was skeered they would scalp her adored;
Behind the front wheel Betsy did crawl,
And there she fought the Injuns with musket and ball.

6. The alkali desert was burning and bare,
And Isaac's soul shrank from the death that lurked there:
"Dear Old Pike County, I'll go back to you."
Said Betsy, "You'll go by yourself if you do."

Red River Valley

Slowly rolling

1. From this val - ley they say you are go - ing, _____ We will
2. Won't you think of the val - ley you're leav - ing? _____ Oh, how

miss your bright eyes and sweet smile, For they say you are tak - ing the
lone - ly, how sad it will be, Oh __ think of the fond heart you're

sun - shine, _____ That bright - ens our path - way a - while. _____
break - ing, _____ And the grief you are caus - ing me. _____

Git Along, Little Dogies

Intro

As I was out rid - in' one mor - ning for plea - sure_____ I spied a young cow - boy a - rid - in' a - long. His__ hat was thrown back and his spurs were a -

jin - gling, and_ as he was rid - in' he was sing - in' this_ song: Yip-pee

Chorus:

ti - yi - yo, git a - long lit - tle do - gies. It's your mis -

C7   F

for - tune 'tain't none o' my own. Yip-pee ti - yi - yo, git a -

G   C   C7   F   G   C   *Verse (fine)*

long lit - tle do - gies, you know that Wy - o - ming will be your new_ home. When

Love Songs

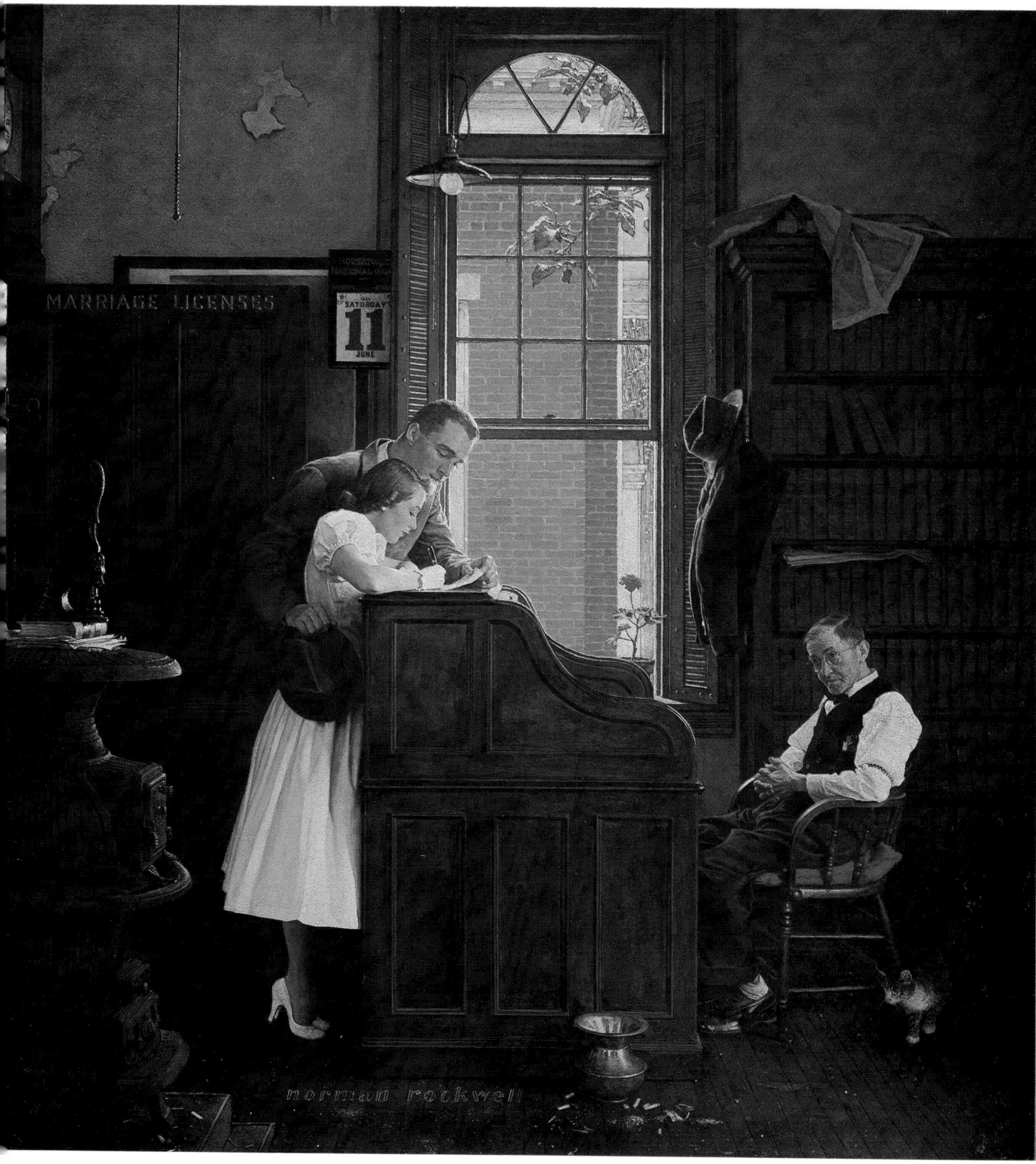
MARRIAGE LICENSES
SATURDAY
11
JUNE
norman rockwell

Scarborough Fair

Sweet Genevieve

Words by George Cooper
Music by Henry Tucker

1. Oh Gen - e - vieve I'd give the world To live a - gain the love - ly past. The rose of youth was dew - im - pearled; But now it with - ers in the blast. I see thy face in ev - 'ry dream, My wak - ing thoughts are full of thee; Thy

glance is in the star-ry beam That falls a-long the sum-mer sea.

Chorus: Oh Gen-e-vieve, Sweet Gen-e-vieve, The days may come, the days may go, But

still the hands of mem-'ry weave The bliss-ful dreams of long a-go.

2. Fair Genevieve, my early love,
   The years but make thee dearer far!
   My heart shall never, never rove,
   Thou art my only guiding star.
   For me the past has no regret,
   Whate'er the years may bring to me;
   I bless the hour when we first met,
   The hour that gave me love and thee.

Oh, Promise Me

Words by Clement Scott
Music by R. de Koven

Oh, prom-ise me that some day you and I Will

take our love to-geth-er to some sky Where we can be a - lone, and faith re -

might - y mu - sic to our ver - y souls; No love less per - fect than a

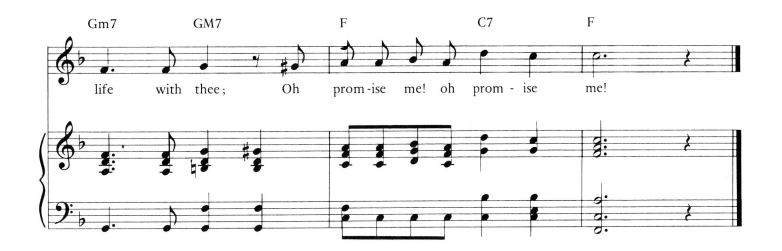

life with thee; Oh prom-ise me! oh prom - ise me!

Sunday, Monday, or Always

Words by Johnny Burke
Music by Jimmy Van Heusen

Copyright © 1943 (Renewed) by Dorsey Bros. Music, a Division of Music Sales Corp., New York, and Burke and Van Heusen, a Division of Bourne Company, New York. All Rights Reserved. Used by Permission.

Aura Lee

Words by W. W. Fosdick
Music by George R. Poulton

1. As the black-bird in the spring, 'Neath the wil-low tree, _____

Sat and piped, I heard him sing, Sing-ing Au-ra Lee.

Au - ra Lee, Au - ra Lee, Maid with gol-den hair,

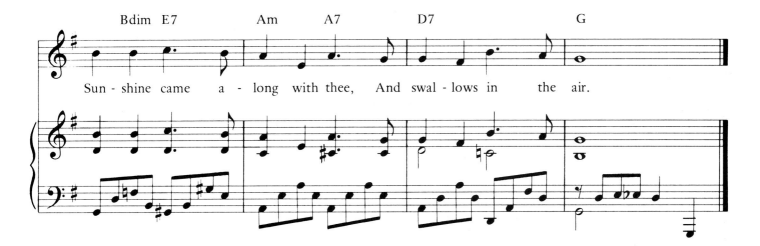

Sun - shine came a - long with thee, And swal - lows in the air.

2. Take my heart and take my ring,
   I give my all to thee,
   Take me for eternity,
   Dearest Aura Lee!
   Aura Lee, Aura Lee,
   Maid with golden hair,
   Sunshine came along with thee,
   And swallows in the air.

3. In her blush the rose was born,
   'Twas music when she spake,
   In her eyes, the light of morn,
   Sparkling, seemed to break.
   Aura Lee, Aura Lee,
   Maid with golden hair,
   Sunshine came along with thee,
   And swallows in the air.

4. Aura Lee, the bird may flee
   The willow's golden hair,
   Then the wintry winds may be
   Blowing ev'rywhere.
   Yet if thy blue eyes I see,
   Gloom will soon depart,
   For to me, sweet Aura Lee
   Is sunshine to the heart.

Daisy Bell

Words and music by Harry Dacre

131

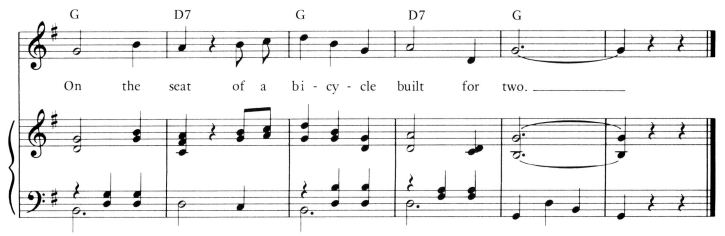

On the seat of a bi-cy-cle built for two. _____

3. I will stand by you in "wheel" or woe,
Daisy, Daisy!
You'll be the belle which I'll ring, you know!
Sweet little Daisy Bell!
You'll take the "lead" in each "trip" we take,
Then, if I don't do well,
I will permit you to use the brake,
My beautiful Daisy Bell!

Black Is the Color

Slowly

1. But black is the col-or _____ of my true love's hair. _____ Her lips are like _____ a

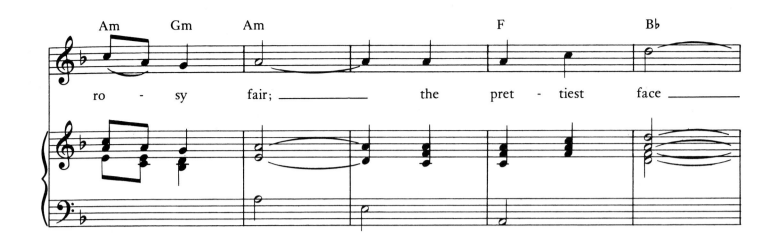

ro - sy fair; _____ the pret - tiest face _____

_____ and the neat ___ est hands, _____ I love the

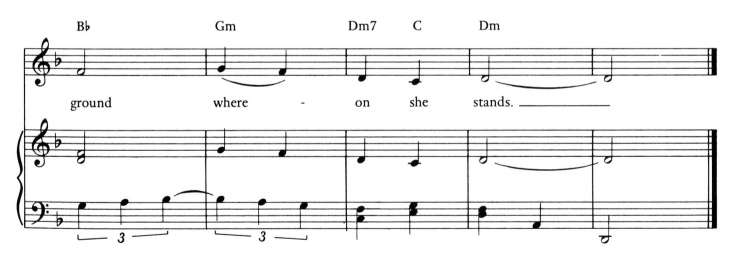

ground where - on she stands. _____

2. I got to the Clyde for to mourn and weep,
   But satisfied I never sleep;
   I'll write to you in a few short lines,
   I'll suffer death ten thousand times.

3. I love my love and well she knows.
   I love the ground whereon she goes.
   If you no more on earth I see,
   I can't serve you as you have me.

My Bonnie Lies over the Ocean

Greensleeves

Green - sleeves was my heart of gold,__ And who but my la - dy Green - sleeves.

2. I long have waited at your hand
To do your bidding as your slave,
And waged, have I, both life and land
Your love and affection to have.

3. If you intend thus to disdain
It does the more enrapture me,
And even so, I will remain
Your lover in captivity.

4. Alas, my love, that yours should be
A heart of faithless vanity,
So here I meditate all alone
Upon your insincerity.

5. Ah, Greensleeves, now farewell, adieu,
To God I pray to prosper thee,
For I remain thy lover true,
Come once again and be with me.

Down in the Valley

Beautiful Dreamer

Words and music by Stephen Foster

1. Beau - ti - ful dream - er, wake un - to me,
2. Beau - ti - ful dream - er, out on the sea,

Star-light and dew - drops are wait - ing for thee. _____ Sounds of the rude world
Mer-maids are chant - ing the wild Lor - e - lei, _____ O - ver the stream - let

heard in the day,
va - pors are borne,

Lulled by the moon - light have all passed a
Wait - ing to fade at the bright com - ing

Jeanie with the Light Brown Hair

Words and music by Stephen Foster

1. I dream of Jean-ie with the light brown— hair,
2. I long for Jean-ie with the day - dawn— smile,

Borne, like a va - por, on the sum-mer's air. I see her trip-ping where the
Rad - iant in glad - ness, warm with win-ning guile? I hear her mel - o - dies, like

bright streams play, Hap - py as the dai - sies that dance on her way.
joys gone— by, Sigh-ing round my heart— o'er the fond hopes that die;

Man - y were the wild notes her mer - ry voice would pour,
Sigh-ing like the night wind and sob - bing like the rain,

Man - y were the blithe birds that
Wail -ing for the lost one that

war - bled them o'er; I dream of Jean - ie with the
comes not a - gain; I long for Jean - ie and my

light brown— hair, Float - ing, like a va - por, on the soft sum - mer air.
heart bows— low, Nev - er more to find her where the bright wa - ters flow.

But Beautiful

Words by Johnny Burke
Music by Jimmy Van Heusen

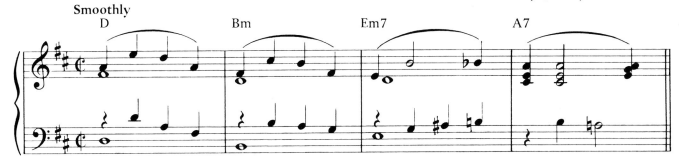

Who can say what love is? Does it start _____

in the mind _____ or the heart? _____

Copyright © 1947 (Renewed) by Dorsey Bros. Music, a Division of Music Sales Corp., New York, and Burke and Van Heusen, a Division of Bourne Company, New York. All Rights Reserved. Used by Permission.

think-ing   if   you   were mine   I'd   nev-er   let   you   go   And   that would be   But

Beau-ti-ful   I   know. _____   Love   is   know. _____

151

I Love You Truly

Words and music by Carrie Jacobs Bond

Andante con amore

I love you tru - ly, tru - ly, dear, Life with its sor - row, Life with its tear, Fades in - to dreams when I feel you are near, For I love you tru - ly, tru - ly

Songs of Faith

Amazing Grace

blind but __ now I see. _____ 'Twas
hour I __ first be - lieved. _____

2. Through many dangers, toils and snares,
   I have already come.
   'Tis grace that brought me safe thus far,
   And grace will lead me home.

3. How sweet the name of Jesus sounds,
   In a believer's ear.
   It soothes his sorrows, heals his wounds,
   And drives away his fear.

4. When we've been there ten thousand years,
   Bright shining as the sun,
   We've no less days to sing God's praise,
   Than when we first begun.

Go Tell It on the Mountains

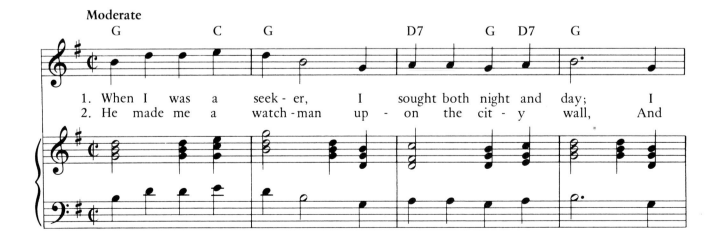

1. When I was a seek - er, I sought both night and day; I
2. He made me a watch - man up - on the cit - y wall, And

asked the Lord to help me, And He showed me the way._____
if I serve him tru - ly, I am the least of all._____

Chorus:

Go tell it on the moun-tains, O-ver the hills and ev-'ry where;__

Go tell it on the moun - tains that Je - sus Christ__ is born.

3. He made me a watchman
   Upon the city wall,
   And if I am a Christian,
   I am the least of all.

4. And, lo, when they had seen it,
   They all bowed down and prayed;
   Then traveled on together
   To where the babe was laid.

Kum Ba Yah

Chorus:

Kum - ba - yah, my Lord, kum - ba - yah, Kum - ba -
yah, my Lord, kum - ba - yah. Kum - ba - yah, my Lord, kum - ba -
yah, Oh, Lord, _ kum - ba - yah. _

All God's Children Got Shoes

4. I got a song, you got a song,
   All God's children got songs.
   When I get to heaven gonna sing my song,
   Gonna sing all over God's heaven, *etc.*

5. I got wings, you got wings,
   All God's children got wings.
   When I get to heaven gonna put on my wings,
   Gonna fly all over God's heaven, *etc.*

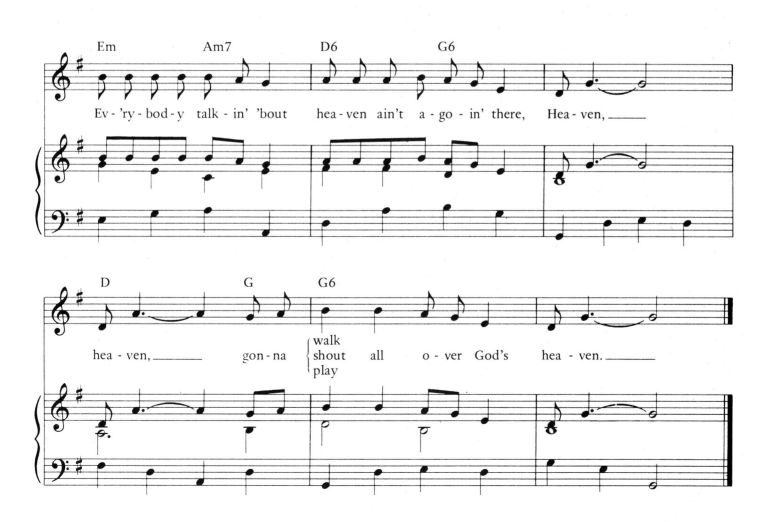

Ev-'ry-bod-y talk-in' 'bout hea-ven ain't a-go-in' there, Hea-ven,_____ hea-ven,_____ gon-na { walk / shout / play } all o-ver God's hea-ven._____

When the Saints Go Marching In

Swing Low, Sweet Chariot

Chorus:

Swing low, sweet char - i - ot___ Com-in' for to car- ry me home,

Swing low, sweet char - i - ot,___ Com-in' for to car-ry me home.

Verse

1. I look'd o - ver Jor - don an' what did I see,___
2. If you get there before I do,___

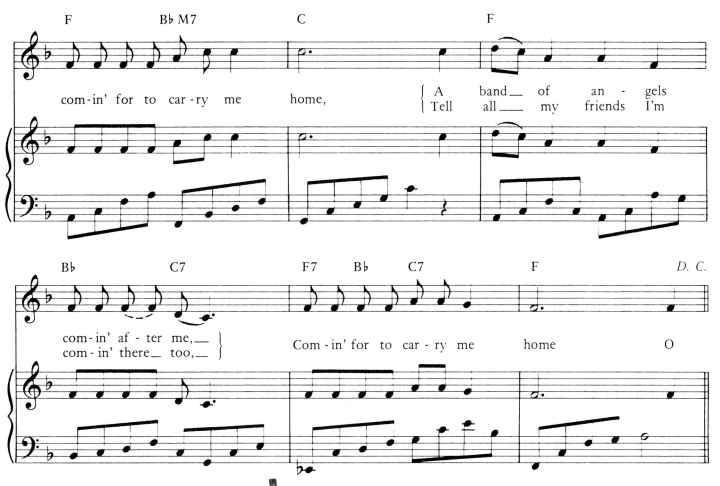

3. The brightest day that ever I saw,
   Comin' for to carry me home.
   When Jesus washed my sins away,
   Comin' for to carry me home.

4. I'm sometimes up and sometimes down,
   Comin' for to carry me home.
   But still my soul feels heaven bound,
   Comin' for to carry me home.

5. I never went to heaven, but I've been told,
   Comin' for to carry me home.
   The streets in heaven are paved with gold,
   Comin' for to carry me home.

167

Sometimes I Feel like a Motherless Child

long way from home, a long way from home. True believ - er, true believ - er, a long way from home, a long way from home.

Nobody Knows the Trouble I've Seen

3. One day when I was walkin' along,
   Oh, yes, Lord;
   The sky opened up and love came down,
   Oh, yes, Lord.

4. What makes old Satan hate me so,
   Oh, yes, Lord;
   He had me once and had to let me go,
   Oh, yes, Lord.

5. I never shall forget that day,
   Oh, yes, Lord;
   When Jesus washed my sins away,
   Oh, yes, Lord.

We Gather Together

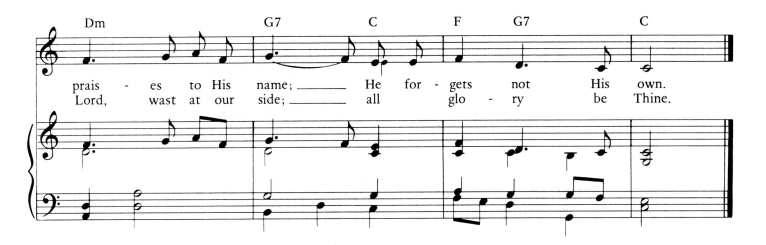

prais - es to His name; _____ He for - gets not His own.
Lord, wast at our side; _____ all glo - ry be Thine.

3. We all do extol thee, Thou leader triumphant,
   And pray that Thou still our Defender will be.
   Let Thy congregation escape tribulation;
   Thy Name be ever praised! Oh Lord, make us free!

Courtesy Massachusetts Mutual Life Insurance Company

Now the Day Is Over

Words by Sabine Baring-Gould
Music by Joseph Barnby

1. Now the day is o - ver, Night is draw-ing nigh;
2. Je - sus, give the wea - ry Calm and sweet re - pose,
3. When the morn-ing wa - kens, Then may we a - rise

Sha - dows of the eve - ning Steal a - cross the sky.
With thy tend - 'rest bless - ing, May our eye - lids close.
Pure and fresh and sin - less In Thy ho - ly eyes.

Holidays

Joy to the World

Words by Isaac Watts

177

sing,   And _ hea - ven and hea - ven and na - ture   sing.
joy,   Re - peat,   re - peat___ the sound - ing   joy.

3. He rules the world with truth and grace,
    And makes the nations prove
    The glories of His righteousness,
    The wonders of His love.

Silent Night

Music by Franz Gruber

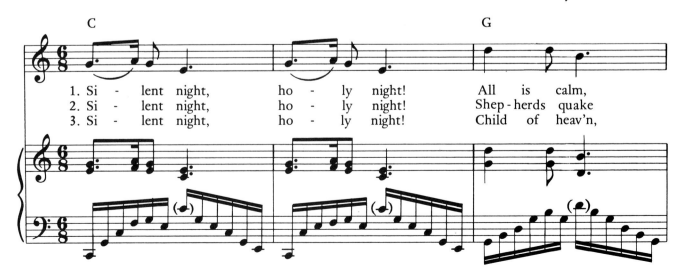

1. Si - lent night,   ho - ly night! All is calm,
2. Si - lent night,   ho - ly night! Shep - herds quake
3. Si - lent night,   ho - ly night! Child of heav'n,

Oh Come, All Ye Faithful

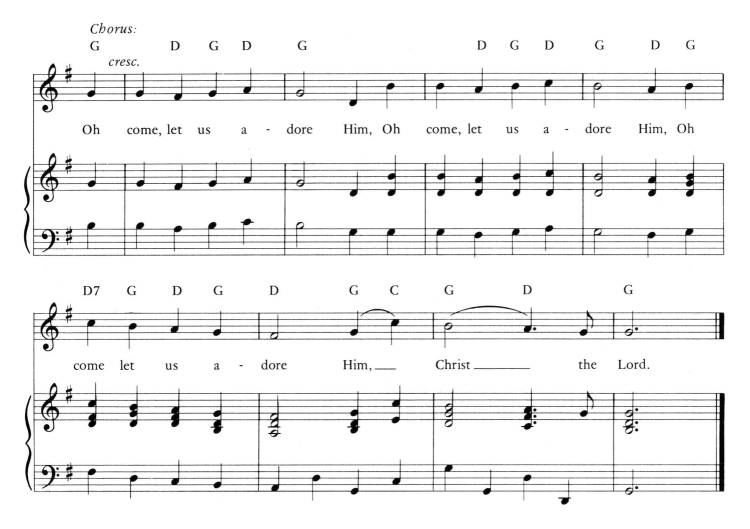

3. Yea, Lord, we greet thee, born this happy morning,
   Jesus, to Thee be glory giv'n;
   Word of the Father, now in flesh appearing:
      Oh, come, *etc.*

4. *Adeste fideles, laeti triumphantes;*
   Venite, venite in Bethlehem:
   Natum videte, Regem angelorum:
   Venite adoremus, venite adoremus,
   Venite adoremus Dominum.

Over the River

Lively

1. O - ver the ri - ver and through the woods, To grand - mo - ther's house we
2. O - ver the ri - ver and through the woods, To have a first - rate
3. O - ver the ri - ver and through the woods, And straight through the barn - yard

go; _____ The horse knows the way to car - ry the sleigh, Through the
play; _____ Oh hear the bells ring, "Ting - a - ling - ling!" Hur -
gate, _____ We seem to go ex - treme - ly slow It

white and drift - ed snow. _____ O - ver the ri - ver and
rah for Thanks-giv - ing Day. _____ O - ver the ri - ver and
is so hard to wait. _____ O - ver the ri - ver and

through the woods, Oh how the wind does blow! _____ It
through the woods, Trot fast my dap - ple gray! _____ Spring
through the woods, Now grand - mo - ther's cap I spy! _____ Hur -

stings the toes And bites the nose, As o - ver the ground we go. _____
o - ver the ground, Like a hunt - ing hound! For this is Thanks - giv - ing Day. _____
rah for the fun! Is the pud - ding done? Hur - rah for the pump - kin pie! _____

Up on the Housetop

Words and music by Benjamin R. Hanby

1. Up on the house, no de - lay, no pause,
2. Look in the stock - ings of Lit - tle Will,

Clat - ter the steeds of San - ta Claus;
Ha! is it not a glo - rious bill?

Down thro' the chim - ney with
Ham - mer and gim - let and

3. Snow-white stocking of Little Nell,
   Oh, pretty Santa, cram it well!
   Leave her a dolly that laughs and cries,
   One that can open and shut its eyes.

4. Pa, Ma, and Uncle and Grandma too,
   All, I declare, have something new;
   Even the baby enjoys his part,
   Shaking a rattle, now bless his heart.

The Twelve Days of Christmas

1. On the first day of Christ-mas my true love gave to me, A par - tridge in a pear tree.

2. On the sec - ond
3. On the third } day of Christ - mas my true love sent to me,
4. On the fourth

2.3.4. Two tur - tle doves, } and a par - tridge in a pear tree.
3.4. Three French hens,
4. Four call - ing birds,

(Sing in reverse order for verses indicated)

Halloween Song

Quick but mysterious

Gob-lins and witch-es ride on a broom, Ghost-ly sha-dows steal 'round the room, to-night. To-night is Hal-low-e'en. _____

Light up the pump-kins, dress in a sheet, Scare ev-'ry bo-dy you hap-pen to meet to

night. To - night is Hal - low - e'en. _____

It Came upon a Midnight Clear

Words by Edmund H. Sears
Music by Richard S. Willis

1. It came up-on__ a mid - night clear, That glo - rious song__ of
2. Still through the clo - ven skies they come, With peace - ful wings__ un -

old.__ From an - gels bend - ing near the earth, To
furled,__ And still their heav'n - ly mu - sic floats, O'er

touch their harps__ of gold.__ Peace on the earth,__ good -
all the wea - ry world.__ A - bove its sad__ and

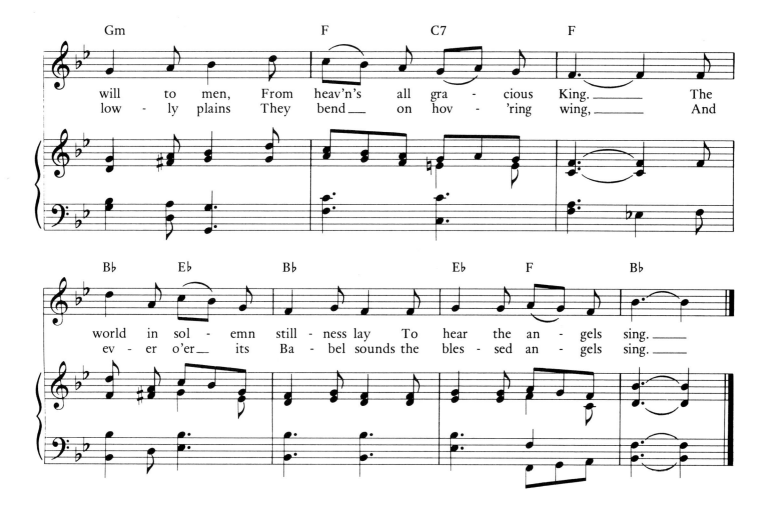

will to men, From heav'n's all gra - cious King. _____ The
low - ly plains They bend __ on hov - 'ring wing, _____ And

world in sol - emn still - ness lay To hear the an - gels sing. _____
ev - er o'er __ its Ba - bel sounds the bles - sed an - gels sing. _____

3. O ye, beneath life's crushing load
   Whose forms are bending low,
   Who toil along the climbing way
   With painful steps and slow
   Look now! for glad and golden hours
   Come swiftly on the wing;
   O rest beside the weary road
   And hear the angels sing.

4. For lo! the days are hastening on,
   By prophet bards foretold,
   When with the ever-circling years
   Comes round the age of gold;
   When peace shall over all the earth
   Its ancient splendors fling;
   And the whole world give back the song
   Which now the angels sing.

On the First Thanksgiving Day

On the first Thanks - giv - ing day Pil - grims went to church to pray,

Thanked the Lord for sun and rain, Thanked Him for the fields of grain.

Now Thanksgiv - ing comes a - gain; Praise the Lord as they did then,

Thank Him for the sun and rain, Thank Him for the fields of grain.

The First Noel

1. The first No - el the an - gels did sing Was to cer - tain poor shep - herds in fields as they lay; In fields where they lay keep - ing their

2. They looked up and saw a Star
   Shining in the East, beyond them far,
   And to the earth it gave great light,
   And so it continued both day and night.

4. Then enter'd in there wise men three,
   Full rev'rently upon their knee,
   And offer'd there in His presence,
   Their gold and myrrh and frankincense.

3. This star drew nigh to the northwest,
   O'er Bethlehem it took its rest.
   And there it did both stop and stay,
   Right over the place where Jesus lay.

Jingle Bells

Words and music by James Pierpont

Gaily

1. Dash - ing through the snow, in a one - horse o - pen sleigh,
2. Day or two a - go, I thought I'd take a ride, And

O'er the fields we go, Laugh - ing all the way; Bells on bob - tail ring,
soon Miss Fan - nie Bright was seat - ed by my side; The horse was lean and lank, mis -

Mak - ing spir - its bright, Oh, what fun it is to sing a sleigh - ing song to - night.
for - tune seemed his lot, He got in - to a drift - ed bank, and we, we got up - sot.

Songs of
Social Concern

DO UNTO OTHERS
AS YOU WOULD HAVE THEM
DO UNTO YOU

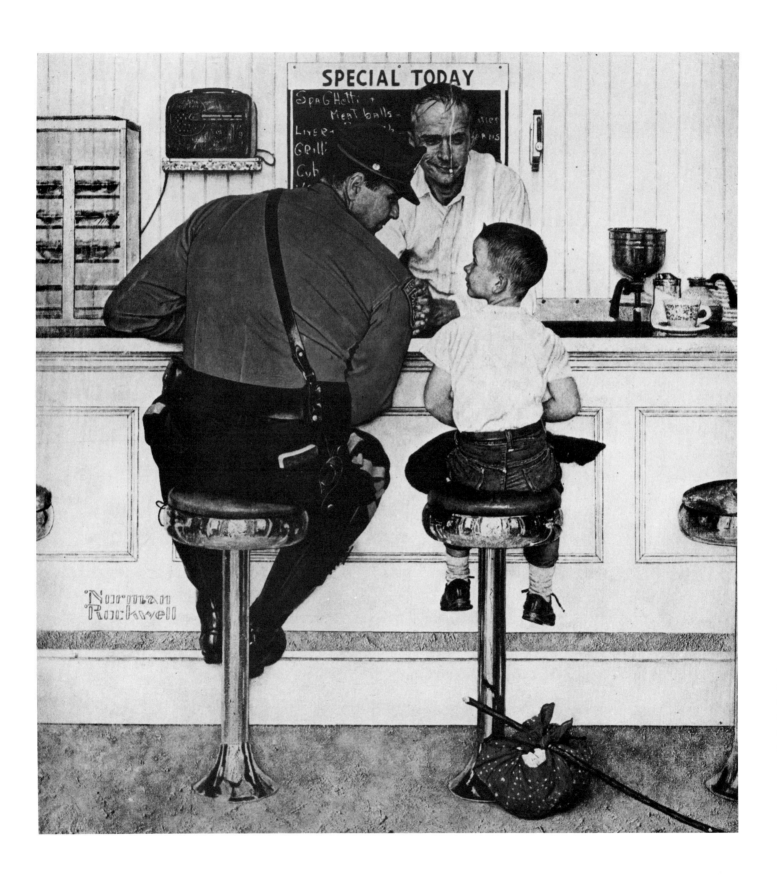

We're Tenting Tonight

Words and music by Walter Kittredge

Slow

1. We're tent - ing to - night on the old camp - ground,
2. We've been tent - ing to - night on the old camp - ground,

Give us a song to cheer Our wear - y hearts, a
Think-ing of days gone by, Of the loved ones at home that

song of home, And friends we love so dear.
gave us the hand, And the tears that said "Good - bye!"

Go Down, Moses

Tell old _____ Pha - roah ___ To let my peo - ple go.

3. The Lord told Moses what to do,
   Let my people go,
   To lead the Hebrew children through,
   Let my people go.

4. O come along Moses, you won't get lost,
   Let my people go,
   Stretch out your rod and come across,
   Let my people go.

5. Your foes shall not before you stand,
   Let my people go,
   And you'll possess fair Canaan's Land,
   Let my people go.

6. We need not always weep and mourn,
   Let my people go,
   And wear these slavery chains forlorn,
   Let my people go.

Down by the Riverside

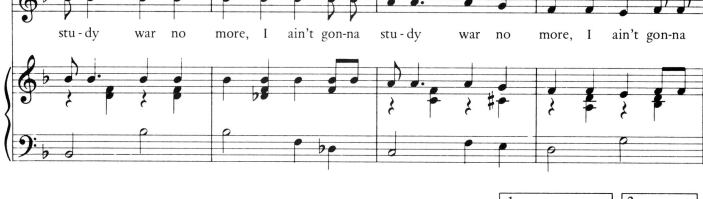

3. Gonna put on my starry crown,
   Down by the riverside, down by the riverside,
   Down by the riverside.
   Gonna put on my starry crown,
   Down by the riverside,
   And study war no more.

4. Gonna put on my golden shoes,
   Down by the riverside, down by the riverside,
   Down by the riverside.
   Gonna put on my golden shoes,
   Down by the riverside,
   And study war no more.

Patriotic Songs

SESQUI·CENTENNIAL·CELEBRATION
OF·THE·SIGNING·OF·THE
DECLARATION·OF·INDEPENDENCE

Norman
Rockwell

America

Words by Samuel Francis Smith

My coun - try, 'tis of thee, sweet land of li - ber - ty,

Of thee I sing. Land where my fa - thers died, Land of the

pil - grims' pride; from ev' - ry __ moun - tain - side, Let __ free - dom ring.

Battle Hymn of the Republic

Words by Julia Ward Howe

March

1. Mine eyes have seen the glo - ry of the com - ing of the Lord; he is tramp - ling out the vin - tage where the grapes of wrath are stored; He hath loos'd the fate - ful light - ning of His

2. I have seen Him in the watch - fires of a hun - dred circ - ling camps; They have build - ed Him an al - tar in the ev - 'ning dews and damps; I can read His right - eous sen - tence by the

John Brown's Body

(Sung to the tune of "Battle Hymn of the Republic")

1. John Brown's body lies a-mouldrin' in the grave,
   John Brown's body lies a-mouldrin' in the grave,
   John Brown's body lies a-mouldrin' in the grave,
   But his soul goes marching on.

2. The stars above in heaven are a-lookin' kindly down,
   The stars above in heaven are a-lookin' kindly down,
   The stars above in heaven are a-lookin' kindly down,
   On the grave of old John Brown.

3. He captured Harper's Ferry with his nineteen men so true,
   He frightened Old Virginia till she trembled through and through,
   They hanged him for a traitor, they themselves the traitor crew,
   But his soul goes marching on.

4. Well, he's gone to be a soldier in the army of the Lord,
   Well, he's gone to be a soldier in the army of the Lord,
   Well, he's gone to be a soldier in the army of the Lord,
   But his soul goes marching on.

Chorus
   Glory, glory hallelujah,
   Glory, glory hallelujah,
   Glory, glory hallelujah,
   His soul goes marching on!

The Caissons Go Rolling Along

Words and music by Brig. Gen. Edmund L. Gruber

1. O - ver hill, o - ver dale, We have hit the dus - ty trail, And those
2. To the front, day and night, Where the dough - boys dig and fight, And those

cais - sons go rol - ling a - long. _____ In and out, hear them shout: "Coun - ter
cais - sons go rol - ling a - long. _____ Our bar - rage will be there, fired

march and right a - bout," As the cais - sons go rol - ling a - long. _____
On the roc - ket's flare As the cais - sons go rol - ling a - long. _____

218

The Star-Spangled Banner

Words by Francis Scott Key

1. Oh say can you see, by the dawn's ear - ly light, what so
2. Oh the shore dim - ly seen through the mist of the deep, where the

proud - ly we hailed at the twi - light's last gleam - ing? Whose broad
foe's haugh - ty host in dread si - lence re - pos - es, What is

stripes and bright stars, thro' the per - il - ous fight, O'er the ram - parts we
that which the breeze, o'er the tow - er - ing steep, As it fit - ful - ly

America the Beautiful

Words by Katherine Lee Bates
Music by Samuel A. Ward

With dignity

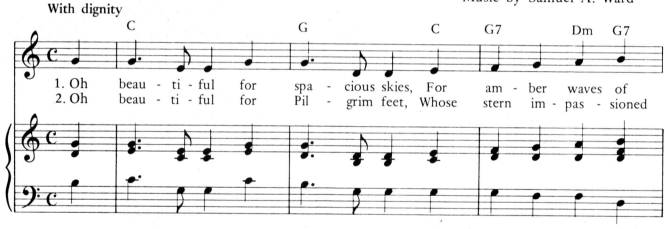

1. Oh beau-ti-ful for spa-cious skies, For am-ber waves of
2. Oh beau-ti-ful for Pil-grim feet, Whose stern im-pas-sioned

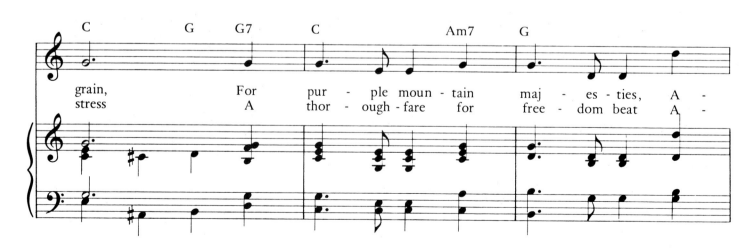

grain, For pur-ple moun-tain maj-es-ties, A-
stress A thor-ough-fare for free-dom beat A-

3. Oh beautiful for heroes proved
 In liberating strife,
 Who more than self their country loved,
 And mercy more than life.
 America! America!
 May God thy gold refine,
 Till all success be nobleness,
 And every gain divine.

4. Oh beautiful for patriot dream
 That sees beyond the years,
 Thine alabaster cities gleam,
 Undimmed by human tears.
 America! America!
 God shed his grace on thee,
 And crown thy good with brotherhood
 From sea to shining sea.

The Landing of the Pilgrims

Words by Felicia Hemans

Moderately

1. The break-ing waves dashed high On a stern and rock-bound coast, And the
2. Not as the con-quer-or comes, They, the true-heart-ed, came; Not

woods a-gainst a storm-y sky Their gi-ant branch-es tossed; And the
with the roll of stir-ring drums,And the trum-pet that sings of fame; Not

hea-vy night hung dark The hills and wa-ters o'er, When a
as the flee-ing come, In si-lence and in fear; They

band of ex - iles   moored their bark On the   wild New Eng - land   shore.
shook the depths of the des - ert gloom With their hymns of lof - ty   cheer.

Marines' Hymn

on the sea.____ First to fight for right and
take a gun.____ In the snow of far - off
lost our nerve.____ If the Ar - my and the

free - - dom and to keep our hon - or
nor - - thern lands and in sun - ny tro - pic
Na - - vy ev - er looked on hea - ven's

clean, ____ We are proud to claim the ti -
scenes, ____ You will find us al - ways on the
scenes, ____ They would find the streets are guard -

tle of U - ni - ted States Ma - rines. ____
job, the U - ni - ted States Ma - rines. ____
ed by U - ni - ted States Ma - rines. ____

Fun and Games

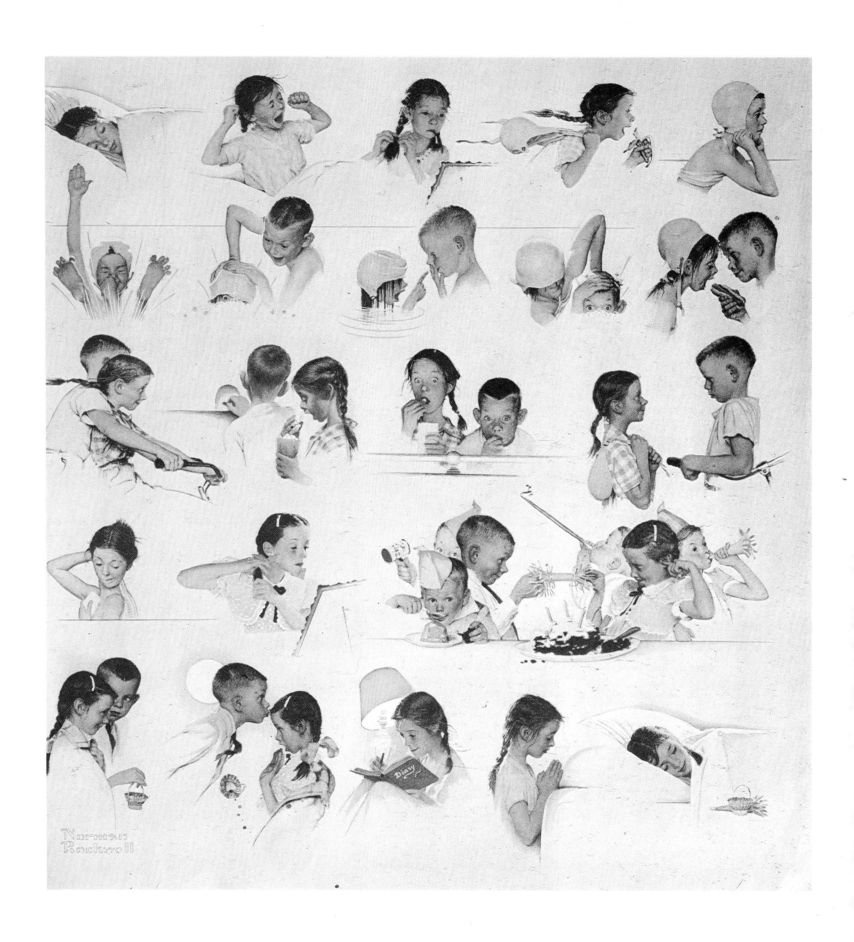

Oats, Peas, Beans, and Barley Grow

3. Waiting for a partner,
   Waiting for a partner,
   Open the ring and take one in
   While we all gaily dance and sing.

She'll Be Comin' Round the Mountain

moun-tain, She'll be com - in' round the moun-tain when she comes._____

hors-es, She'll be driv - in' six white hors-es when she comes._____

3. Oh, we'll all go out to meet her when she comes,
   Oh, we'll all go out to meet her when she comes,
   Oh, we'll all go out to meet her,
   Oh, we'll all go out to meet her,
   Oh, we'll all go out to meet her when she comes.

4. Oh, we'll all have sugar and dumplings when she comes,
   Oh, we'll all have sugar and dumplings when she comes,
   Oh, we'll all have sugar and dumplings,
   Oh, we'll all have sugar and dumplings,
   Oh, we'll all have sugar and dumplings when she comes.

5. We'll be singin' hallelujah when she comes,
   We'll be singin' hallelujah when she comes,
   We'll be singin' hallelujah,
   We'll be singin' hallelujah,
   We'll be singin' hallelujah when she comes.

Skip to My Lou

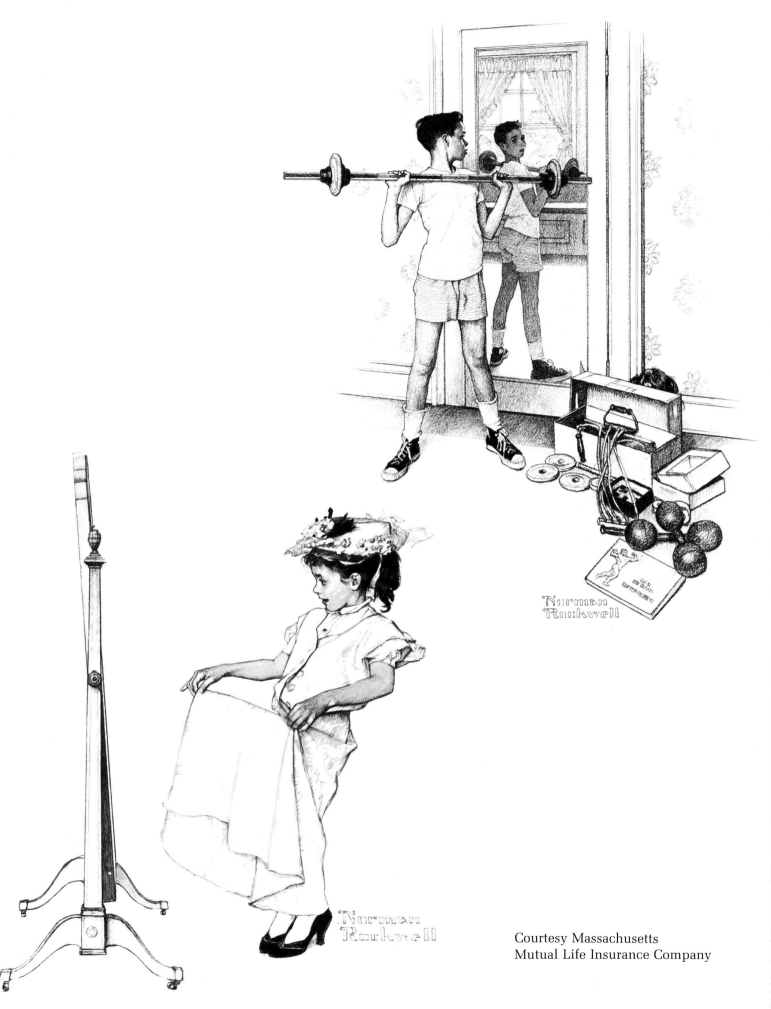

Courtesy Massachusetts
Mutual Life Insurance Company

This Old Man

3. "three," "knee"
4. "four," "door"
5. "five," "hive"
6. "six," "sticks"
7. "seven," "till elev'n"
8. "eight," "gate"
9. "nine," "spine"
10. "ten," "over again"

Old MacDonald Had a Farm

Here a chick, there a chick, eve - ry - where a chick, chick,
Here a quack, there a quack, eve - ry - where a quack, quack,

Alouette

Lively
Chorus:

A - lou-et - te, gen-tille a - lou-et - te, A - lou-et - te, je te plu - merai.

Solo: *Chorus:*   *Solo:*   *Chorus:*

1. *Je*   *te plu - me-rai la tête,*   *Je*   *te plu-me-rai la tête,*   *Et*   *la tête, Et*   *la tête.*   *Oh!*
2. *Je*   *te plu - me-rai le bec,*   *Je*   *te plu-me-rai le bec,*   { *Et*   *le bec, Et*   *le bec,*   *Oh!*
                                                         Et   *la tête, Et*   *la tête.* }

Je te plumerai: (I will pluck your:)
1. *La tête* (head)
2. *Le bec* (beak)
3. *Le nez* (nose)
4. *Le dos* (back)
5. *Les pattes* (feet)
6. *Le cou* (neck)

242

The Green Grass Grew All Around

and the green grass grew all a-round.　　Oh, the green grass grew all a-

round, all a-round, and the green grass grew all a-round.　　round.

Courtesy Massachusetts Mutual Life Insurance Company

The Bear Went over the Mountain

1. The bear went o - ver the moun - tain, the bear went o - ver the moun - tain, The
2. He saw an - oth - er moun - tain, he saw an - oth - er moun - tain, He

bear went o - ver the moun - tain to see what he could see.
saw an - oth - er moun - tain and that's what he could see.

Guitar Chord Diagrams

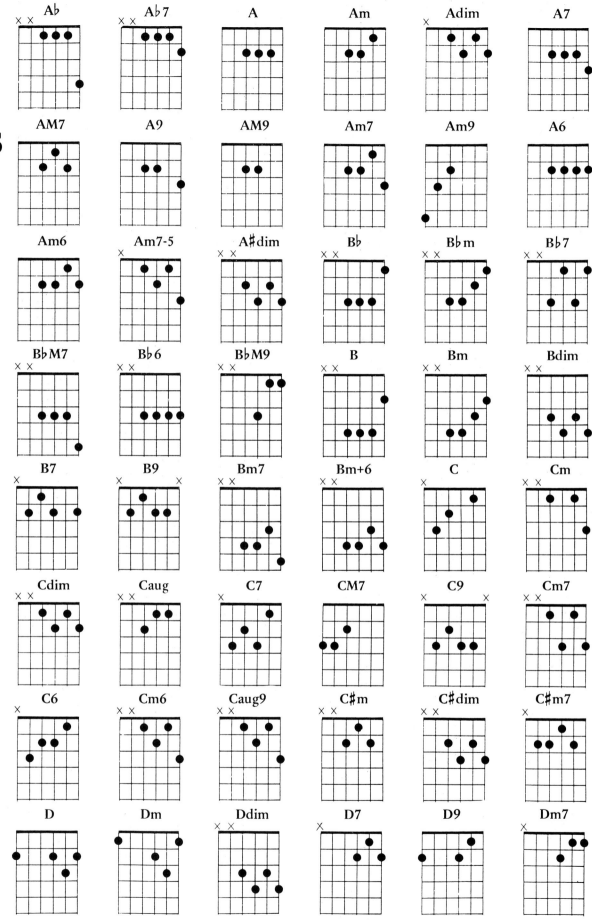

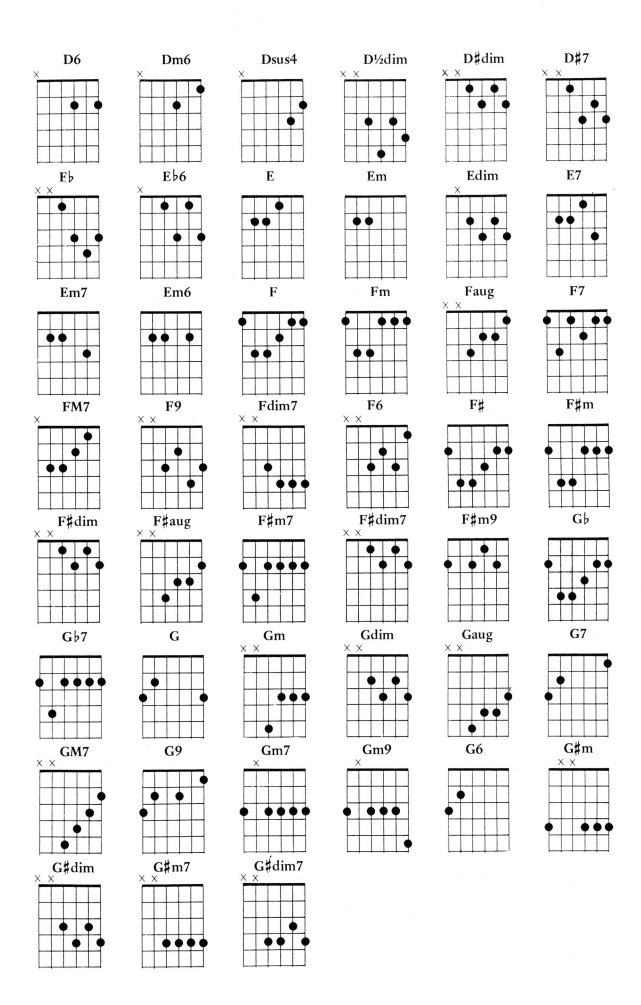

Title Index

Stephen Dydo is a composer living in New York City. His compositions include works for chorus, orchestra, and chamber and vocal ensembles, as well as computer and electronic works. In addition to composing, he is completing work on a computerized music editing and printing system. He has an MA and a DMA in composition from Columbia University, and has been awarded a Fulbright research grant, the Bearns prize, and a BMI award.

Randa Kirshbaum, who also lives in New York City, arranges music professionally and is a composer and pianist as well. Her compositions include music for a Greek play, a children's operetta, and chamber pieces. She has a BA from Swarthmore College and an MA in composition from Columbia University, and is compiling a collection of unpublished folk songs.